I dedicate
this book to my
loving wife, Vici;
and great thanks again
to Kay Grynyer who has
struggled nobly to type it
and cope with my mistakes!

An environmentally friendly book printed and bound in England by
www.printondemand-worldwide.com

This book is made entirely of chain-of-custody materials

Ramblings of a Much-Hugged Vicar

Stumbling further ?? towards integrity.

– HUGH MADDOX –

www.fast-print.net/store.php

RAMBLINGS OF A MUCH-HUGGED VICAR
Copyright © Hugh Maddox2014

A catalogue record for this book is available from the British Library

ISBN 978-178456-121-5

First published 2014 by
FASTPRINT PUBLISHING
Peterborough, England.

Introduction

Several people have asked for a sequel to *Tales of a Huggable Vicar*, so here goes.

I had a variety of reactions to the book. Some people really did not like it – and told me so! These were all good friends. However, I was much encouraged by other responses – one lady read it through much of the night and immediately ordered six more copies. Others stood in front of me in the street to tell me how they had been helped by reading it, especially when they had read of difficult and testing experiences similar to their own. I often pretended to be hurt by friends who had not bought it, and worse, friends who <u>had</u> bought it, glanced at it ......and never thought it worth reading!

I said to one friend,

"I'm worried that some people may find the book - too snobby – some will find it – too religious – and, well others – too coarse."

"Naturally," he replied, "You are!".

So, I have tried to learn and repent, but I hope you will find this random account of episodes, thoughts and poems entertaining and, hopefully, helpful.

Not everyone liked the title, "Tales of a Huggable Vicar", but nobody's alternative suggestion indicated the necessary three aspects : stories, sauciness and religion. Anyhow, whenever I showed somebody the flyer, they chuckled – and often gave me a hug on the spot! To attract the more serious minded, I added the sub-title, Stumbling towards integrity.

I wonder what I learned through writing my life story? I am now more fully aware of the difference between the lives and attitudes of most people on the one hand and the privileged circumstances and social attitudes of my childhood and teen years on the other. It was good that I had the calling to be a priest, as it led me to share some of the emotions and attitudes of others.

Sadly, these days, well into retirement, I am not in daily contact with such a variety of people as in my working life. Some reprehensible prejudices from my childhood begin to peep through again, but, at least, I am aware of them!

The other day I needed the words of a hymn to give to somebody – as I can't type, and certainly don't have a computer, I wrote it by hand. I was delighted to discover again the old truth that a student remembers the words which he has written himself, slowly, with his own pen. The words of hymns are often wonderful, profound poetry, and although we have sung them all our lives, the full possibility of their meaning can still elude us.

With this in mind, I have scattered around in this book some of my favourite verses. Many of them are addressed to God and can be used as a prayer. I have taken the liberty of spacing out the words and phrases so that you can savour what they are revealing.

Mother

When our son was in his early thirties he moved into a flat. My mother was staying with us at the time, and I found her at the breakfast table, with tears of laughter pouring down her face.

"Mother, what on earth are you laughing about?!"

She replied,

"I had said 'Jamie, here's £20 for you, to buy yourself a toaster, and make sure it is a good one", and I wagged my finger at him in mock seriousness. He said,

"Thank you, Grannie, and when I burn the toast, I will think of you, Grannie.

"How is that, Jamie?"

"In the Crematorium, Grannie"

She loved it and she continued to shake with laughter.

Later in the year, she stood with him in a furniture shop, offering to buy him an armchair. With a twinkle in her eye, she asked him,

"How will you think of me now, Jamie?"

"At rest, Grannie!"

Aged 107 and very frail, my mother moved to a kindly, gracious Nursing Home, Marley House, in the pretty village of Winfrith. She had been there for 5 months; I looked in one Saturday morning and could hardly wake her; in the afternoon my sister, nephew, and niece drove from London to see her – she appeared to be barely conscious, but on hearing them discussing Aunt Elsie's home in Edinburgh, she woke and corrected them, "No, it was Walker Street"!

I looked in on Sunday morning, and immediately saw that she had just died, having "turned her face to the wall", as the Bible often says. I called a young nurse who was very shocked, as she had given her a drink only a few minutes before. My daughter made a very wise comment, "Dying is a very private thing, and some people want nobody around." I suddenly realised why relatives are so often distressed when a parent dies just a few minutes after they had left the ward, intending to return very soon.

I had the unusual privilege of saying the Prayer of Commendation at the very moment for which it was written. With my hand on her still warm forehead, I said to her:

"Mother
Go forth upon thy journey from this world, O most
    Christian soul,
In the peace of Him in whom thou hast so strongly
    believed.
In the name of God the Father, who created thee,

In the name of Jesus Christ, who suffered for thee,
In the name of the Holy Ghost, who strengthened
thee.
May angels and archangels, and all the armies of the
heavenly host come to meet thee,
May all the saints of God welcome thee,
May thy portion this day be in gladness and peace,
and thy dwelling in Paradise.
Go forth upon thy journey, O Christian soul.
In the name of Jesus Christ, our Risen Lord.
Amen.

The nurses were in tears. I left – to take a christening in Lulworth – death and new life.

I wanted to have some sort of service for her in Wareham, for the sake of my friends who had met her here. We decided on a happy arrangement – a Communion Service, with hymns, in the little Saxon Church of St. Martin-on-the-Walls. Her coffin was piped in and placed parallel to the altar, so that the great themes of the Eucharist seemed to enfold her, love, sacrificial, redeeming, self-offering, forgiveness, eternity.. We put out forty chairs and another thirty stood.

Her funeral was in her parish church near Lloyd Square in London. The family gathered behind the hearse outside her house and a piper led the way. As often happens with the family member organising a funeral, my mind was so active with all the details, and my immediate reaction had been one of relief – relief that all her frustration of blindness, deafness and weakness was now over – that no grief surfaced. On hearing the first wail of the pipes that all changed – and I did not check my weeping till we reached the church. The procession wound slowly round the Square and across a busy road, people coming out of their homes and shops to listen and watch. My ten year old grandson, Caspar, darted out of the procession to grab some lumps of sugar from a table outside a pub.

My mother had asked for a simple service, "as there will not be many there, as all my generation have passed away ...." But, in her eighties, she had taught in the Sunday School (as well as putting a little hot water in her cold morning bath) and delighted the little children with her Bible stories; so with many of the congregation present, as well as friends and relations of all ages, we were nearly two hundred.

At the end of the service I asked everybody to stand on the pavement in silence – so often people start talking at this point – the pipes started up again and the hearse slowly turned the corner, the sound of the pipes gradually fading away behind the great trees of the Square.

My mother had given instructions, "When the service is over, drive me into the garage, go back into the Church, have something to eat and drink, on me, and meet each other; and take me to the Crematorium afterwards". I think this was wise – it gave everybody the chance to see the coffin, which is so important for cousins, nephews and nieces, close friends as well as the immediate family; denied that opportunity, it is hard for them to fully take in the fact of death – they are denied that necessary catharsis.

The organist at the Crematorium wore a loose-fitting purple silk shirt, rather like the organist in the Vicar of Dibley. I asked him for some Scottish music and he gave us Loch Lomond, the sad song of the Jacobite Highlander to be executed in Carlisle the following morning; he would travel home on the fairy road under the ground, while his fellow prisoner, due to be released, would trudge over the hills to Scotland – "but me and my true love will never meet again on the bonnie, bonnie banks of Loch Lomond."

We walked out to "Wull ye no' come back again."

No lack of catharsis there!

With some of the family present, we buried her ashes in Arran, in a dignified light, cardboard heart-shaped casket, covered in dried leaves (easy to carry on the train). We met by the ancient, ruined chapel of Kilbride, high above the village of Lamlash; one grandson carried the casket and another placed it in the grave. A hefty young Island piper, in full military dress, eight feet to the top of his bearskin, led the long walk through the graveyard, playing "Flowers of the Forest", that haunting tune composed after the disastrous battle of Flodden, when the good King

James IV, many of the nobility and soldiers of Scotland, were killed.

The family grave overlooks the sea, Holy Isle and the hills. My father's inscription reads, "A lovely life," my brother Colin's, "He loved this Island, and was much loved", and my mother's, "A gallant little lady", which was my father's favourite description of her.

As we stood in silence there was an overwhelming sense of deep sadness at the end of many generations of family times on our beloved Island.

Turkey

Browsing through the magazine for the National Trust for Scotland, I saw an advertisement for a cultural coach tour of western Turkey, reduced from nearly £800 to £200. My Lowland ancestors said, "Ye must not miss a barrrgain – book up nooo."

My Highland ancestors, extravagant and loving travel, agreed. My wife Vici, would have found it too physically demanding; we are going to Guernsey instead, so I had to find a companion to share a bedroom to bring down the cost. Half the human race would have been considered unsuitable, so I had to find another bloke to come with me. Tragically my first choice died, my second choice was too busy, but my third agreed immediately.

I had first met David Marshall when I was taking a funeral and he was acting as a bearer, carrying the coffin. Actually he had offered to play the trumpet, as he was a first class musician. He came sailing with me and loved to tell how he missed picking up the buoy for the third time and how in my most classy voice, I shouted. "Oh, for God's sake, David!

Years later when his wife died, I got to know him better.

David had been brought up on a small farm on Bodmin Moor and ended up as the Director of Music of the Coldstream Guards. At the end of the Queen's Annus Horribilis, David was conducting the orchestra for the Christmas Carol Service in the Guards Chapel, and so was standing very near the Queen. Seeing her looking very sad, he broke protocol, went up to her, took her hand and said, "I do hope you have a happy Christmas, your Majesty."

He was an ideal companion with endless stories of Army musical life, all around the world. We talked deeply, giving each other due respect, but pulled each other's legs remorselessly.

Some of the hotels were magnificent and I enjoyed saying to some of our more right-wing fellow travellers, "Isn't it wonderful that an old couple, on benefits, if they saved carefully, could stand in this expensive place with us – unthinkable for their grandparents." In the following discussion somebody quoted "But the sun shines on the righteous….."

"Do you know how the quote ends?"

"No, tell me."

".….and the unrighteous alike,"

and a distinguished, elderly Catholic finished Jesus' words,

"and the rain falls on the just and the unjust."

Shock on the faces of our respectable fellow travellers.

Again and again Jesus denounced the self-righteous – and indeed there is something shocking in St. Paul's passionate belief that we are saved by God's free gift of grace and not by our respectable blameless lives. It is shocking because it seems to undermine the belief in hard work and morality, but it is profoundly true. Thank God!

On the edge of the classical ruins of the great city of Ephesus was Mary's house, the legendary home of Our Lady. Although it was not a Pilgrimage, I thought some of our party might like some prayers; fifteen joined me in an ancient, semicircular room under the open sky. We thanked God for Mary, for the loving upbringing which she will have given her son; for we can only give love if we have already received it. The adolescent Jesus will have been guided by Joseph (his stepfather?) and totally loved by "my Father in heaven". We remembered the pain of Mary as her twelve year old son was so wrapped up in religion that he ignored the terrible anxiety he caused his parents, as he stayed behind in Jerusalem. She may have felt further rejection years later, when she wanted to speak to him; he was surrounded by his fan club; they told him,

"Your mother and brothers are outside, asking to speak with you."

Jesus gave the devastating reply,

"Who is my mother, and who are my brothers?" and stretching out his hand towards his disciples, he said,

"Here are my mother and my brothers! For whoever does the will of my Father in heaven is my brother, and sister and mother."

Her greatest agony, of course, was still to come, when "a sword was to pierce her own soul, also", as she saw her son nailed to the wood.

In heaven, she is very close to all fathers and mothers who have lost a son or a daughter.

I am reminded of Studdert Kennedy's poem in the First World War.

A MOTHER UNDERSTANDS

Dear Lord, I hold my hand to take Thy Body, broken here for me;
Accept the sacrifice I make, my body, broken, there, for Thee.
His was my body, born of me, born of my bitter travail pain,

And it lies, broken on the field, swept by the wind
    and the rain.
Surely a Mother understands Thy thorn-crowned
    head,
The mystery of Thy pierced hands – the Broken
    Bread.

There in Turkey, we stood in the traditional home of Our Lady, and Catholic, Protestant, Muslim, alike, we said the Scriptural words,

Hail, Mary, full of grace;
The Lord is with thee.
Blessed art thou among women,
And blessed is the fruit of Thy womb, Jesus.
Holy Mary, Mother of God,
Pray for us sinners
Now, and at the hour of our death.
Amen

We kept silence.

A Turkish official had been standing by, making signs. I am glad that I did not pay any attention to him until our service was over, because he beckoned to me, and waving his hand, said,,

"No permit, no permit"!

Turkey is a secular country, but with 98% Muslim population. You are allowed to pray in a mosque, on your own, or, with special permission, with up to twelve others. I apologised but the official refused to shake my hand, until the Iranian ladies in our party merrily charmed him, and he reluctantly agreed!

Those prayers were much appreciated by many in our party, so on our last morning I crept around the tables at breakfast, hissing,

"Prayers, Room 215, 10.30 a.m."

Our worshippers sauntered casually down the hotel corridor, and glancing around, entered our room. We all felt a tiny bit of what persecuted Christians, down through the centuries, and today, must feel, knowing that they are worshipping together – in danger of their lives.

• • •

I was overtaken by two boys on bikes as I walked along the pavement to Wareham; it could have been dangerous. As I walked, I wondered what I should have said. I saw them mucking about by the bridge – an opportunity! I smiled, and in a cheerful voice, said,

"Hello! I saw you cycling along the pavement and ...."

Before I could finish, they blurted out,

"Oh, but we didn't hit you ....!"

I stopped them, and carried on,

"Yup, I think it is safer than riding on that narrow road, - but supposing I had stumbled to the left just as you had swerved to the right, I might have knocked you onto the road under the wheels of a car."

"Well, what should we do then?" – still defensive.

Staying with my pleasant, uncritical voice(!), I suggested that they ring their bells as they approached.

"But we ain't got no bells!"

Indeed very few modern bikes do have a bell, and not any other means of communication, in spite of the amazing gadgets of modern communication! One friend of mine was killed by a bicycle speeding silently down a hill while he was crossing the road. So I said,

"Why don't you give a shout as you come near anybody on the pavement?"

"Orr right".

I continued walking up the street, and heard a great cheerful shout as two bikes shot by!

I felt very smug and pleased with myself. I guess that if I had shouted at them they would have just given me a lot of lip, and ridden more furiously.

• • •

I was in my old parish with two ladies, senior in church and village, and we were talking sadly of the departure of my successor as Vicar, One of them said,

"It's a shame he's going – he hasn't had his fingers in the till, - or been chasing women; (pause) unlike you (another pause) – and you didn't have your fingers in the till!

The three of us fell about spluttering with laughter; they both had known me well for twenty years, and it was not a serious allegation, but they had seen my roving eye in the years when I was on my own

I felt that this kindly, saucy laughter about my human frailty was parish life in the dear old C. of E. at its best.

• • •

I was taking the funeral of Denis Wallace-Jones in Kingston Church. We had already had the burial, so the part most painful for the family was behind us. Denis was a wonderful, kindly, relaxed jovial fellow; he had served in the Navy, and so we started the funeral with the great, strong hymn, "Eternal Father, strong to save, whose arm doth bind the restless wave........." The organ was being repaired, so the undertaker brought in an electric organ. Terence Arden, the organist, was not familiar with it, so to give more volume for the second verse, he pressed one of the switches; it produced the same tune, but with jazz accompaniment. We only just managed to finish the last verse with straight faces.

"Denis would have loved that," I said; the whole congregation collapsed with laughter; and so were relaxed enough to take in the address and the rest of the service. Laughter can help tears flow.

During my retirement, I have often become painfully aware of the many mistakes I had made in my working life as a Vicar, especially when I see other clergy doing exactly the same!

In my forties I had wanted to get rid of the Book of Common Prayer, in spite of the fact that the congregations found it helpful. I thought that new translations of the Bible were necessary and scorned the criticism of new liturgies for lacking in poetry; I wish we had stuck to the Revised Standard Version of the Bible, used in the 1950's and in all our theological lectures. Sometimes it clarifies the meaning but it usually keeps the balance of a sentence, with the powerful word coming at the end. I remember the comment of one journalist when the New English Bible first came out – he had noticed that he had read several chapters at one session without having to stop to absorb any powerful saying. Only strong, imaginative phrases stay in the mind, phrases which if heard over and over again we learn by heart. Too much choice, too much spontaneity, mean that nothing stays in our conscious or subconscious spirit.

These days I wince at the recollection of the way I used to take services. Even though I might have greeted every parishioner at the church door, when I had come from the vestry, to some magnificent organ music, I would destroy the moment by welcoming everybody, as if to my home, instead of it being God's house in which many of the congregation had worshipped years before I appeared and would continue to do so long after I had gone!

Occasionally I had succumbed to the belief that I needed to "improve" the service with interruptions and false jollity, even making a meal out of the notices. In contrast I recall Douglas Fulton, our minister on Arran, giving out the "intimations " just before the sermon – "There will be a coffee morning in the church hall at ten o'clock on Tuesday" – no embellishment, no encouraging people to come and bring a friend, no promise of how much we would enjoy it! Instead, I would emphasise certain items which already appeared in the written notice sheet. In all, I think we clergy are inclined to patronise our congregation in many irritating ways! Apart from the notices and sermons, the object is to lead the people in listening to God and speaking to Him; the Vicar is not talking to the congregation all the time.

In the last few years, I have come to fully appreciate the value of liturgy, the set words of the service. They are beautiful, poetic, profound; they are the prayer of the Church; when I am full of doubt, or depressed, I can join in, saying them with confidence, even if I do not <u>feel</u> them at the present moment. They express what I <u>want</u> to believe, what I <u>want</u> to hope for; strange to say, the liturgy removes from me what I once heard described as "the burden of sincerity". I love the story of some devout

Christians who were on an expedition, and an Orthodox monk was one of the party. The others were surprised that each evening he hopped into bed without saying his prayers. When questioned, he replied,

"Oh, I have no need, because I am a member of the Community and they are praying the prayers of the church back at the monastery."

I find this a healthy corrective to our Western individualism. He took his membership of his community far more seriously than we would. To be a member of a physical body, a hand or a foot is to literally belong to the whole – this is supremely true in our "membership" of the Body of Christ – something far more profound, more mystically true, than being a "member" of the local cricket club.

In my sermon I usually spoke with a loud voice, as I did in reading the prayers, but, even so, some of the congregation said that they could not hear me. I have since realised that I was probably dropping my voice at the end of the sentence, when often the final word is the important one and should be given full stress. All too often, we adopt an apologetic "parson's voice" in both reading and speaking.

It is only lately that I have hit upon a helpful way of responding to someone at the church door, thanking me for my sermon. I may ask,

"Did you find anything especially helpful in it for you?

As always, a question can help a person put his own new thoughts into words, - and we usually remember our own words more than other people's, don't we? If a man is asked what was said in a group discussion, we often hear him reply,

"Well, I said that ...."

By putting a new thought into our own words it becomes part of us.

In taking a service, I try to be aware of the full humanity of Christ, linking it with the needs of all us ordinary folk, using plain, non-theological language; but also, I hope to be aware of the awe, the mystery of the love of God, profound mystery which is far beyond human comprehension or human language. Many people today are going to Cathedral services – the soaring building, the superb singing, the beauty of the Church's liturgy, the profound, limitless symbolism and power of the sacrament of the Body of Christ, all go beyond words and take the worshipper out of himself to become aware of the presence of the living God. The very lack of subjective feelings in the presentation of the service, paradoxically, can lead me to weep at the revelation of God's love for me, or my poor response, or the sadness of human tragedy.

I warmly recommend the film, "Of Gods and Men" – you can buy the DVD. It is the true story of eight, French, Benedictine monks in Algeria in the 1990's, it has English sub-titles. The photography is superb – the hot Algerian countryside, both lush and barren, the village and the villagers, and above all, the slow filming of the magnificent varied faces of the Brothers. There is much silence and the haunting sound of the Brothers singing the liturgy – somewhat reminiscent of Taize. It is set against the background of the rising violence of Islamist extremism; the Brothers, prayerfully, personally, honestly debate whether to stay to help the villagers, or leave to save their lives. I have watched it over and over again; it is both humbling and inspiring.

• • •

Last year I took the christening of Dora, the daughter and grandaughter of dear friends in Cornwall. I was just about to take the baby in my arms, when the photographer came and stood right in front of me. I was so enraged that I shook my fists in the air and shouted,

"It makes me so angry!!"

Fortunately, Pippa, the baby's granny, gave me a warm, amused smile, so that I could "calm down and carry on". After the service both the photographer and I rushed over to each other and apologised..........and the family must have forgiven me, because I am taking the wedding this year.

I have just taken another wedding, and the cheerful photographer readily agreed that he would only take one photo in front of the bride and groom. I told him of my rage during the christening and he said,

"If I do that, tell me to bugger off."

During the first hymn he was moving around by the altar, taking shot after shot. With my back to the wedding couple, I glared at him and mouthed, ~"Bugger off!" He retreated, only to emerge again, snapping away with his large camera behind me while the bride and groom exchanged their vows. I could tell from their eyes that they were distracted, - so before we came to the prayers I went over to him and hissed,

"GO AWAY – you have ruined it!!"

Having got what he wanted, he disappeared and I recovered composure.

Only later did I realise that he was standing next door to the video camera – so when the film is shown the screen will suddenly be filled with the distorted face of a very angry little man.

I had also christened Dora's cousin, Myrtle, now three. I was chatting with her and then went out into the garden.

"Granny, where's God?" she asked.

"In heaven, darling".

"Then how can He have christened me?!"

With my beard and white robe, toddlers often mistake me for Jesus – it's only an outward appearance, I fear. Sometimes I nearly cause an accident by standing, robed, at the bottom of our drive, causing a startled driver to swerve on seeing Jesus.

Overheard in a Post Office: a young man, the father of a three-year old son and a baby daughter, told his friend,

"When my son saw the baby's cot was empty, he asked,

"Has the baby gone back in Mummy's tummy?!"..........perhaps that is what he wanted.

Like many others, I am not happy with the new baptism service which demands affirmative answers to such questions as "Have you accepted Christ as your Saviour?" – much too narrow a question for the fringe people who come.

After celebrating Holy Communion, I no longer use the traditional prayer, "May the souls of all the faithful departed rest in peace – and rise in glory!"

Instead, I say, "May the souls of ALL the departed rest in peace – and rise in Glory!"

An old, valued and godly friend is suffering from deep depression. When he arrived I gave him a hug and he began to crumble and weep. We talked and he looked so stricken with despair that my eyes filled with tears.

I said,

"Let's stand up and I will give you another huig".

I held him and he sagged in my arms: after he had sat down he said,

"Sorry, I have just farted!"

I fell about with laughter, and he sat there with a broad grin on his face. A good form of counselling?!

• • •

From the hymn, 'O worship the Lord in the beauty of holiness'

Low at his feet lay
Thy burden of carefulness:
High on his heart
He will bear it for thee,
Comfort they sorrows
And answer they prayerfulness,
Guiding they steps
As may best for thee be.
Fear not to enter
His courts in the slenderness
Of the poor wealth
Thou wouldst reckon as thine;
Truth in its beauty,
And love in its tenderness,
These are the off'rings
To lay on his shrine.
These, though we bring them
In trembling and fearfulness,
He will accept
For the name that is dear;
Mornings of joy give

For evenings of tearfulness,
Trust for our trembling
And hope for our fear.

One day, last summer, I was sitting in our garden discussing his theological paper with John Porter, another retired priest. We were not arguing about it, but exploring its implications; however, I sensed that we were missing something important, so I said,

"John, let's just be quiet for a moment – and see if we are missing anything."

He agreed; I took several deep breaths, slowly letting out all tension, dropping my shoulders, opening my hands on my knees, letting go of all the control of my mind, all cerebral domination – so that I could be open in both feeling and thinking.

Totally unexpectedly, I was overwhelmed by a sense of deep sadness ......followed immediately by a sense of personal inadequacy; I then felt real warmth around my shoulders. At this moment, my brain did click in, as I remembered how John Wesley had had a similar experience – (not that I am like him!).

I then heard, quite distinctly, a voice saying,

"My child,......my child"

Spoken with a voice both strong and tender, infinitely understanding.

I knew that it was my Father God reassuring me, as if He were saying,

"Hugh, my son, I made you and I gave you talents which you have used, a good mind, a loving heart and a vivid imagination, and you have used them well. I did not give you much physical courage, self-discipline or dogged perseverance, so don't compare yourself with other people who may appear to have achieved more than you. You have helped more people in a quiet way than you realise."

I found this immensely reassuring, and later I remembered some words of my mother, who had died the previous year. It was at a time when I had had to leave a thriving parish, and with my famous ancestors in mind I said,

"I hope, Mother, that you don't regret my failure."

She said, with complete surprise,

"Of course not, darling; all I want is for you to be happy!"

Perhaps, in heaven she was prompting God to say the same thing!

Who knows....................?

There may be a psychological explanation for my experience in the garden, it may have been something like schizophrenia, where the sufferer hears voices. Of course I am fully aware of these possible explanations, but the effect was the same, and I have continued to remember and claim those affirming words, "My Child, My Child."

I heard that voice as clearly as if John, sitting beside me, had spoken, although he heard nothing.

The only other occasion was just after my father had died; I was running down the paddock regretting how little I had seen of him lately, and called out,

"Sorry, Father, sorry!"

I then saw his face, on my right, smiling broadly and saying,

"It's all right, it's all right!".............and I knew it was.

Many people have had similar experiences. The next Sunday morning, after the voice in the garden, I told the congregation about the voice of my Father God, saying, so lovingly, "My Child, My Child", - it is a message, not just for me, but for everybody. Somebody said, "You were inspired this morning"; I hope my words had touched his heart. It has never, been quite so powerful in the retelling.

• • •

In his forceful, gutteral voice our Turkish tour guide told us of a bride and groom who could only afford one horse to take them on their honeymoon. After a mile or two their combined weight made the horse stumble and fall to the ground.

"First time!" said the groom to the horse.

They mounted and continued on their way. The horse stumbled and fell again.

"Second time!" said the groom to the horse.

They mounted again and continued on their way.

The exhausted horse stumbled once more and fell to the ground.

The groom drew his pistol and shot the horse through the head.

"Oh, the poor thing," cried the bride, "You shouldn't have done that!"

"First time!" said the groom.

• • •

Last year I took a lovely wedding in one of the Purbeck villages. The bride was a doctor, working in a hospital, so many of her guests were from Eastern countries, Buddhist or Hindu by upbringing. There was also a request from Roman Catholics for the service to include a Eucharist. I broke the bread and blessed the wine and invited all to receive. Beforehand, we had wondered whether many would come forward, but to my delight, a majority of the congregation accepted the invitation, with real respect.

Some may question my right to do this, because Confirmation is necessary to receive Communion – and didn't Jesus say, "No man cometh unto the Father but by me."?

However, I now believe that human generosity and openness of heart are closer to the heart of

Christ than restrictive ecclesiastical laws – "The Sabbath was made for man and not man for the Sabbath" was one of Jesus' repeated sayings – and was one of the reasons why the church authorities needed to kill him. I am hoping that I shall not have to receive such drastic treatment.

When people quote Jesus' other saying, 'No man ...." I remind them that these words may not have been spoken by Jesus of Nazareth but are the mystical, poetic interpretation of St. John.

The way of Jesus is the way of death to self and new life received from God – without an end of pride and self-centredness, there is no full humanity. Is this not true in all faiths and all human experiences, whether through the help of a priest, a rabbi, an imam, a guru, or a psychotherapist?

From the lovely Victorian hymn, "Eternal Ruler of the ceaseless round"

We would be one in hatred of all wrong,

One in our love of all things sweet and fair,

One with the joy that breaketh into song,

One with the grief that trembles into prayer,

One in the pow'r which makes thy children free

To follow truth, and thus to follow thee.

• • •

In the town I met an elderly member of a well known local family, walking with a stoop. I asked after his health, and he replied,

"As you can see I am very stiff in my back ....but no longer stiff in the front"!

Poor old man.

Ian Morrison comes from the Outer Hebrides; he spent his holidays with his grandparents in a black house, one of those ancient long, low, thatched cottages, where the family lived in one half and the cattle in the other – when he wanted to go to the loo, he just went next door and peed in the straw; he remembers the gaelic chanting of the Psalms – they have the same haunting, spiritual sound as plainsong, or the chanting of Buddhist monks. After Church one morning Ian noticed that my well-polished shoes were very shiny.

"If you looked at them reflecting up - you could see what you were wearing under the kilt!"

My gradaughter, Nooka, was with me in the garden when Ian and his Chinese wife, May, came for lunch. Nooka had bare feet and Ian told her how he had stayed with his grandparents as a boy and never wore shoes; he told her how he had helped them when they were cutting peat; he would stack it up to dry. What an image for Nooka to share with her grandchildren in years to come!

Last year I stayed with the Campbells of Barcaldine, north of Oban. They took me to the

West Highland games; we gathered on the pier and followed about twenty pipers leading the Highland chiefs, each with a feather in his bonnet, headed by the Duke of Argyll, the Chief of the Clan, with two eagles feathers pointing proudly skywards. We were in the Members Enclosure and were given free whisky, and met many interesting people. The pipes were always playing in the background.

On the train south from Edinburgh a group of exceedingly smart young ladies came down the aisle, immaculate hair styles, fashionable little hats on their heads, neat little bums tightly clothed at my eye level. In stark contrast, in broad Geordie, one of them asked,

• • •

"Is this the right train for Doncaster races?!"

I was walking down the main street of Wareham, talking with a local workman as we went. He is a Jehovah's Witness; he has not had an easy life and we were discussing the bad news coming from all over the world.

"It'll be orr right when the Kingdom of God arrives"..................he said, "but when the fuck is it going to come?!"

This was exactly the same complaint which you find in the Psalms, when the writer bitterly rails against God for allowing his enemies to triumph over him.

G.K.Chesterton was converted to Catholicism. Somebody said,

"Well, the way you live is no great advertisement for the Faith!"

He replied,

"You should have seen what I was like before I converted!"

No answer to that. He wrote the Father Brown detective stories, and also this tough hymn, as relevant today as when he wrote it in the early nineteenth century:

O God of earth and altar,
Bow down and hear our cry,
Our earthly rulers falter
Our people drift and die;
The walls of gold emtomb us,
The swords of scorn divide,
Take not they thunder from us,
But take away our pride.
From all that terror teaches,
From lies of tongue and pen,
From all the easy speeches
That comfort cruel men,
From sale of profanation
Of honour and the sword,
From sleep and from damnation,
Deliver us, good Lord.
Tie in a living tether
The prince and priest and thrall,

Bind all our lives together,
Smite us and save us all;
In ire and exultation
Aflame with faith and free,
Lift up a living nation,
A simple sword to thee.

I took a Remembrance Sunday service in Langton Matravers, originally a quarryman's village near Swanage. It had a small population, but the names were slowly read out of more than thirty young men who had been killed. In those days there were several schools in Langton; only four or five years after these boys had left, they were leading their men over the top into a hail of bullets and shells – the average life-expectancy of a 2nd Lieutenant was only a few weeks. The cynics who mock the senior officers forget the agony they suffered through the sacrifices paid by their sons and nephews.

Some years ago now, I sold my boat, my beloved Cornish Shrimper; but I was introduced to a senior policeman, Tony Nott, who kept his white hulled Shrimper on the river at Wareham, just opposite the Priory Hotel. Since his retirement he often takes me out; I don't have to pay a penny, I don't have to lift a paint brush, I don't have to lie on my back applying anti-foul to the bottom of the boat, I don't even have to lift the anchor – I just sit in the cockpit and steer. Although he had sailed across the Channel in his previous, larger boat, he was new to a Shrimper and generously called me his Sailing Master, reluctantly agreeing to take the risks which I confidently recommended.

Once we took out a Canadian woman family friend of his; she was an experienced and successful sailor – and knew it! Tony told her of my great knowledge of Poole Harbour ....but I stuck the boat fast on thick mud on a receding tide. Fortunately we had a bottle of wine with us. The previous week Tony had stood on the foredeck, anchor in hand, ready to moor for our peaceful picnic; I put the helm down so hard that the boat heeled right over and he was knocked into the water; but he is a good and forgiving man and continues to ask me out regularly.

He has many a tale to tell – he was seconded to Kosovo to supervise the exhumation of bodies from massed graves, to Iraq to advise the police after the invasion, and to Jerusalem. He was the senior detective in Bournemouith, with many gripping stories of evil murderers. He is a committed liberal Catholic, also holding many Right Wing views, so we have many discussions, sometimes going aground because we are talking too much.

• • •

I met somebody who had just read my book, with its references to hunting and to sailing. She said,

"You have mud on your boots and salt in your beard" – I liked that.

Robert Louis Stevenson had written:

Under the wide and starry sky
Dig me a grave and let me lie;
Gladly did I live and gladly die
I lay me down with a will,
The sailor home from the sea,
The hunter home from the hill.

• • •

When I was ordained, fifty years ago, anybody who had been divorced was not allowed to receive Holy Communion without permission from the Bishop and were not allowed to remarry in church. I suppose that the Church maintained this strict attitude in the vain hope of proclaiming the absolute and irrevocable nature of the marriage vows – "for better, for worse, till death do us part" – but, instead, these rules just caused bitterness and resentment.

• • •

In his kindly, human autobiography, *Vets in the Vestry*, the Church of Scotland minister, Alexander Cameron, tells a story about praying for something.

In the Highlands in the nineteenth century the factor of an estate had great power. One of his tenants was usually a contented, cheerful man, but one day the minister met him in the village and said,

"Angus, you're looking gey glum the day; whit's the matter?"

"Och, meenister, it's a terrible thing – the factor is going to pit me oot o'my croft, even though I've paid the rent, - and it was my faither's afore me, and his faither's afore him. Whit am to doo?"

"Oh, Angus, that's a terrible thing, " said the minister, "you'll just have to pray."

"Ay, meenister, its even come to that!" said Angus wearily.

The next week the minister met him again, looking his usual self once more.

"Angus, I'm right glad to see you looking cheerful again. What's happened?"

"Och, meenister, meenister," said Angus happily, "The Lord's the boy, the factor's deid!!"

In a strange way Angus was partly right – I am worried about something – I bring it to my heavenly Father, and try to leave it with Him – every morning I run in to the garden, scantily clad, fling my arms towards the sky, and, one by one throw my worries to Him.

"But how does that help?!" asked one sceptical friend.

"It helps me!" I replied.

Perhaps a few weeks later, I realise that my worrying situation has greatly changed for the better; in that case I go into the garden and raise my arms to heaven in gratitude.

Praying to God for things is not the only purpose of prayer, - to the surprise of many people – it's just as important to thank Him often for the basic gifts of life, food, shelter; it's important to say sorry, to be lost in silent adoration; at the heart of praying is the offering of myself, to be available for God to work through me in the day ahead.

Eternal God and Father
You create us by your power
And redeem us by your love.
Guide and strengthen us by our Spirit
That we may give ourselves
In love and service to one another
And so to you.
Through Jesus Christ our Lord

By loving people, animals and all creation we are loving God, for He is in everybody and everything. So many people scoff at religion, thinking (and often with reason) that we believe there is a person above the sky who interferes with the world either when we ask him or when we deserve it. In contrast, we believe that God is beyond definition, beyond our imagination; we talk to "him" AS IF to a father, because that is helpful ....for us.

I think, that, reluctantly, I have to let go of the idea of a God who can intervene to help me – and this is scary – and believe, instead, that almost anything is possible if I am open to the God who is Love, to inspire both me and others.

Enough of all this ....

Tim Oddy had just gone into Bournemouth Hospital for an operation on his shoulder. He was very impressed that as soon as he was settled in bed, I turned up; we chatted and I gave him a blessing – the Ward went respectfully silent and the Consultant and his Registrar waited quietly in the doorway. I left, feeling very gratified ....but nobody spoke to Tim all day ....either he was a god-botherer who might turn on them..........or he was about to die!

Two Catholic priests were on holiday; they were fully dressed, but not in clerical garb, they were reclining on deck chairs on the beach, when a lovely, topless blonde came out of the sea and greeted them,

"Hello, Father, Hello, Father".

Next morning they took more care and wore teeshirts and Bermuda shorts. The same gorgeous, topless blonde strolled along the beach –

"Hello, Father, Hello, Father!"

Puzzled, they asked,

"But how do you recognise us?"

With a broad smile, she replied,

"You don't recognise me, do you? I'm Sister Mary-Jane!"

I heard this old favourite on 'Vicar's Jokes' on TV – a lovely, unprofessional, naïve series of grinning men and women Vicars, bubbling with glee. There were a whole lot of jokes which I would have loved to repeat ....but I could only just remember one!

During the Depression in the 1930's there was a very poor family. The boy longed to play football with the other boys at school but he had no boots and his mother could not afford to buy any. Before going to sleep, he knelt at his bed and prayed for some football boots. Later that evening a neighbour came round, saying,

"My lad has grown out of these football boots. Would they be any use to your Jimmy?"

His mother gratefully received them, crept into the boy's room and placed them on the end of his bed. In the morning he rushed downstairs, clutching his boots and gleefully shouting,

"Look, Mum, see what God has given me!.............and there wasn't even a hole in the roof!"

Because the boy had asked for God's help, he naturally saw this simple act of human kindness as the work of God – which it surely was, whether the neighbour was religious or not. I only hope that his mother told him the full truth.

I believe that God works in people and through people ....and if we look with expectant eyes we may see miracles all around us.

When I post a bundle of letters I pray about each one – asking for healing for somebody in hospital, thanking God for a good party ....and even when posting a cheque for the gas bill or tax return I can thank God for warmth, food, for hospitals, schools, benefits, security etc.

If I am asking God for help for somebody, or for myself, I try, first of all, to be honest about my own feelings, whether they are of anger, despair, or a longing for healing for somebody I love. God knows I have these feelings, so why try to hide them? So, I start by saying,

"Please, please help!"

Next I have to pull back, be more detached and say,

"But over to You, Father."

I believe that this twofold pattern of intercession is good; it was the prayer of Jesus in Gethsemane. The outcome may be terrible – nothing stops the disastrous growth of the cancer cells and death follows, but if all the family and the dying man have been praying in this way there can grow more quiet acceptance and a sense of peace and less bitterness. I have been humbled to see this many times through the privilege of being a parish priest.

John Bell is a member of the Iona Community. It was founded by the great George MacLeod; inspired by the holy Island it lives out political and personal care in Glasgow and many parts of the world.

MacLeod had broken off a fundraising lecture tour of America to fly to Scotland to give a character reference for a teenager being tried in court for murder. This is one of John Bell's hymns, sung to a lilting tune, and under the title, "Christ's is the world in which we move".

Feel for the people we most avoid,
Strange or bereaved or never employed;
Feel for the women, and feel for the men
Who fear that their living is all in vain.
Chorus:To the lost Christ shows his face;
To the unloved he gives his embrace;
To those who cry in pain or disgrace
Christ makes with his friends a touching place.
Feel for the parents who've lost their child,
Feel for the women whom men have defiled;
Feel for the baby for whom there's no breast,
And feel for the weary who find no rest.
Feel for the lives by life confused,
Riddled with doubt, in loving abused;
Feel for the lonely heart, conscious of sin
Which longs to be pure but fears to begin.
Chorus:To the lost Christ shows his face,
To the unloved he gives his embrace,
To those who cry in pain or disgrace
Christ makes with his friends a touching place.

It is sometimes hard to sing these verses.

• • •

Our Turkish guide told us of a music professor. He was in the middle of teaching his students when a telegram was brought to him. He opened it and in a proud voice told his students,

"This is from the Secretary to the Queen. She wants me to be her Director of Music. I must go and ring him with my obedient acceptance."

He bustled out to the telephone, and on his return found a group of chuckling students gathered round the blackboard. They had written "God save the Queen!"

I have just been to the Albert Hall, for the first time in my life. A lady in Stoborough had been seriously ill in hospital for months; in gratitude for the prayers and visits of many church members she very generously paid for our tickets for a variety concert in aid of research into Parkinson's Disease. The young conductor had just been diagnosed with its first symptoms; the Hall was full, largely with middle-aged and elderly supporters and when he first appeared, five thousand voices cheered like football fans and ten thousand hands clapped a welcome. It was a great experience to be caught up in such enthusiasm. The compere had us in stitches, especially with his quick repartee with members of the audience; but I felt my age with another stand-up comedian – I couldn't hear much of what he said and wasn't amused by what I could hear. The music was terrific and we ended by all singing 'Look on the bright side of life'! It was a great way to end such a concert.

I walked along Knightsbridge and caught the tube to Leicester Square, near St. Martin-in-the-Fields. I was troubled by the contrast between some of the almost obscene opulence flaunted in Knightsbridge, the cars, the shops, the hotels and then the quiet desperation of men sleeping in the doorways. Leicester Square was full of life, light and noise. Young people of every hue and tongue Only a few hundred yards away was my friends' flat, where I was to spend the night – the little street was silent and empty; and even at half-past seven next morning it was quiet, with very few people about – until the throng arrived, hurrying to work; I felt the country bumpkin.

Next morning I walked in Green Park, between Picadilly and Buckingham Palace; I remembered the true?! story of Queen Victoria walking with her beloved husband, Prince Albert. He picked a flower and handed it to the pretty nursery maid who was wheeling the royal pram. The jealous Queen was so angry that she ordered all the flower beds to be dug up – and they have never been replanted.

Crossing the road in Northumberland Avenue I was nearly knocked down by a motor-cyclist hurtling between the stationary traffic. To calm myself I sat in the sun in the Embankment Gardens. With their noble old trees and manicured lawns and only a hundred yards from the thundering traffic it felt remarkably quiet and peaceful. I read a P.G.Wodehouse novel on my kindle; I have mastered the art of turning the pages – the speed at which I am using modern technology is truly amazing. I also noticed a statue of a dignified, bald Victorian man, Samuel Plimsol, with the touching inscription, "Donated in gratitude by men of the sea of all nations." For a moment I was puzzled, until I realised that in earlier years unscrupulous ship owners had dangerously overloaded their ships with too much cargo, liable to cause disaster and loss of life in heavy seas. In many countries today, poor workers struggle for long hours, in appalling conditions for very little or no pay ....and this happens in England as well. Constant vigilance and action is always needed, as the rich get richer and the poor get poorer.

For this short trip to London I had been very organised and booked my return train ticket – with my Old Man's Rail Card it only cost £12 – but I forgot to bring it! At Waterloo Station I had to buy another ticket,

"A Senior Citizen ticket to Wareham, please".................

Nothing happened, and the official said nothing.............till

"Where's your card then?"

At Wareham Station I don't even mention my card – they know me.

I looked in to a small service at St. Martin's and introduced myself to the new Vicar; he didn't know me and had never heard my name; this was the first time I was unknown to the Vicar since I had left St. Marin's forty years ago – sad. Fortunately, that same evening a man saw me outside the church,

"It's Hugh, isn't it?!"

We went and had a bowl of soup together in the Crypt Café – Roger Shaljean had been on the staff with me all those years before.

It was heart-warming to be remembered.

One of Austen William's powerful recollections was of a time when he came down the Vicarage stairs to open the front door. A rather dishevelled man stood on the doorstep – Austen looked at him blankly.

"Austen, do you remember me?"

"No".

"Don't you remember me?".

"No-o".

"Surely, you remember me?"

"No, I'm afraid not".

The man turned away, disappointed and utterly miserable. Austen never forgot his searing shame at the memory of this moment. This came to mind as I rejoiced that Roger Shaljean had remembered me. Re-membered – does this mean his greeting had re-membered me back into the community of St.

Martin's, once again a member of the body of that remarkable, caring church?

I love celebrating the Holy Communion. To keep the action fresh I often think of myself being Peter, the fisherman, telling a group of new Christians what had happened on that remarkable night of the Last Supper. As I break the bread and bless the wine, I say Jesus' own words,

"Do this in remembrance of me"

Anyone who has done any acting knows that while you are on the stage you "live the part" – you are Hamlet or an old woman. Over the years I have asked many men to act the part of Jesus in a Passion Play and I believe it had a profound impression on many of them – it helped them think as Jesus thought and feel as he felt, - from within, as it were.

There are many names for the service, the Mass (from the Latin to go forth), the Eucharist (the Greek for thanksgiving), Holy Communion (in union with church and each other) or the Last Supper, but whatever our understanding, whatever our theology we can be at one with the Eternal Christ with His comfort, His challenge, "Follow me".

A Prayer before a Communion Service:

As the watchman looks for the morning,
even so, do we look for thee, O Christ.
Come with the dawning of the day
and make thyself known to us
in the breaking of the bread,

for thou art our Lord and our God,
For ever and ever.

Yesterday I took the Assembly at the Primary School next door; I told them of blind Bartamaeus. I told the children to close their eyes, stand up and try to move around – of course they all bumped into each other. They sat and I asked them what would a blind man have to do in Jesus' time, if nobody would give him a job? Finally a boy said,

"He'd have to beg."

I got them all to put out their open hands in the begging position – utterly dependent on the generosity of others.

I acted Jesus, walking on the way to Jerusalem, his mind full of what would happen to him there. One half of the school cried out, "Jesus, help me!" and the other half shouted, "SHUT UP!" which only made the blind man cry all the louder, with real desperation, "JESUS, HELP ME!" and the crowd shrieked, "SHUT UP!"

As I was walking in front of them I said one of the most significant words in the Gospels, "Jesus stopped". Although he was so important and so busy – Jesus stopped; – when he heard the desperate cry of the blind man he said,

"How can I help you?" not

"What you must do for me," but "What can I do for you?" and the man said,

"Give me my sight".

Jesus healed him; He still can give us inner sight, if we ask. We then talked about how God can give blind people their sight today, through doctors, hospitals, operations and medicines.

After the Assembly I was with a class of 7 year olds; they had all prepared questions to ask me – much the best and easiest way for me to take a lesson! – I always try to put the question back to them, as did Socrates and Jesus. One said,

"Which do you think are the most important of the Ten Commandments?"

"What do you think?"

"Do not murder," and another piped up,

"Do not steal somebody else's wife".

With sad faces, they all nodded. Poor little mites.

One good question was,

"What did you do as a Vicar?"

Amongst other things, I talked about calling on a family I knew well, where there had been a sudden awful death.

"What do you think is the first thing I do?"

They looked puzzled and then one suggested,

"Do you say, 'Are you O.K.?'" but I held out my hands and said,

"Perhaps, but what did I DO?"

After some prompting from the teacher, one child suggested,

"Give them all a cuggle?"

"Yes," I replied, "I hugged them, as long as they needed."

The discussion went on, considering all sorts of questions and many repeated anecdotes of their great grandparents in the war.

At the end of the lesson one little girl rushed over to me, flung her arms around my neck and gave me a "cuggle"! – immediately followed by two others. I was delighted and only hoped that none of the children told their mothers that "the Reverend Hugh had been hugging little girls"!

It is sad, isn't it, when innocent, spontaneous natural affection could possibly be so misinterpreted? Have we lost a sense of balance and proportion in a society which is so suspicious and sees evil everywhere? I have listened to many people who were abused as children and know of the lasting damage it caused, but all too often the perpetrators were family or close friends. I also worry about the word 'abuse' as it seems to cover everything from being shouted at to rape – and other people usually assume the worst. It is sad, isn't it? Anyhow, I left the School in good spirits, all my worries forgotten and feeling close to my Master – "Let the little children come unto me."

During 2013 I had seen a lot of one of my oldest and closest friends, Roger Musker. His lovely and talented wife, Alison, was increasingly suffering from Altzeimers, and I went to support him. In December he died of a massive heart attack. He had a wonderful family, loving and with many great characters; they asked me to take his funeral in his parish Church. Roger loved the music of Mozart and had written a detailed, meticulously assembled account of all his music. Roger was also a great enthusiast and wonderfully warm in his greeting to everyone. His grandson, William, had sung the solo first verse of "Once in Royal David's City" in the broadcast service of Kings College, Cambridge. Roger had never met the Master of Music, Stephen Cleobury, but, undaunted and with typical warm enthusiasm, Roger sailed through the Choir Vestry after the service, and with hand outstretched, greeted Stephen, proclaiming "I am the grandfather of WILLIAM!" They became firm friends and in spite of his hectic pre-Christmas life, Cleobury came to Roger' funeral to play the organ, bringing a superb singer with him. In the previous Sunday service at Kings, there were prayers for those who had died; just two names were mentioned: Nelson Mandela and Roger Musker. Roger would have been both amazed and highly delighted. Mercifully during the Funeral Service there were moments during music or readings when I could sit in my stall and, with heaving shoulders, let out some of my pent up emotion. A hand came from behind me and rested on my shoulder.

I ended my address by saying,

"By now Roger will have sailed up to the gates of heaven, hand outstretched to greet St. Peter who will have met him with a kindly smile, saying

"Roger, welcome; we've been expecting you; and Wolfgang Mozart is really looking forward to meeting you".

I miss him dreadfully and still can't believe that I will never again pick up the telephone to hear his cheerful voice saying,

"Hugh, it's your old mucker, Roger".

• • •

To decide what you want, and ask God to give it to you –

Sounds to me like the practice of magic.

To offer yourself to God for what He wants you to do – sounds more like Christian prayer.

This thought reminds me of President Kennedy's inspiring speech to the young:

"Ask not what America can do for you,

but what you can do for America."

It led to many thousands of young men and women going to serve the poor overseas.

This is the prayer for Maundy Thursday, the night of the Last Supper, when Jesus astonished his followers by washing their dusty, sweaty feet:

Heavenly Father,
Your son Jesus Christ has taught us
that what we do for the least of our brothers and
 sisters
we do for him:
give us the will to be the servant of others
as he was the servant of all,
who gave up his life and died for us,
even Jesus Christ, our Lord.

• • •

Roland Walls was a most learned and deeply prayerful monk. One day he was having lunch in a pub with a friend, and the man's little boy. After lunch they all went to the Gents, the little boy standing between the two men. He peered over towards Roland and in his piping little voice said,

"Why is your thing so much smaller than Daddy's?"

Quick as a flash, Roland replied,

"Because Daddy's has so much more work to do!"

History does not relate how the conversation went after that.

A little girl had a young brother; one day she asked her mother,

"Mummy, I know that the baby came out of your tummy, but how did it get there?"

Her mother explained the facts of life to her and with a horrified look on her face, the little girl said,

"So do you mean that Daddy did that to you twice?!"

• • •

On a Sunday morning, through the open windows of the School next door, we heard the sound of an electric guitar and loud singing of a modern hymn – the Baptists at worship. A few minutes later the good Lord would have to strain his ears to hear their prayers, nearly drowned out by the fruity party voices of all our guests drinking in our garden – these drunken Anglicans!

My Uncle, Moray McLaren, was a brilliant mimic and story teller, a merry and devout Catholic. Brought up in the Church of Scotland and converting to Catholicism, he was at home with strong authoritarian doctrines and belief. Like many Scots he enjoyed teasing members of the Scottish Episcopal Church, mockingly known as the English Church, and considered to be wishy-washy in doctrine, and favoured by the landowners and those enjoying good living – a false picture, I assure you.

He told of an ecumenical fishing trip in a boat on a Highland loch – the Catholic priest, Father McDonald, the minister, the Reverend Donald McLeod, and the well fed Dean of the Episcopal Cathedral, the Very Reverend James Stewart.

After a morning's fishing they anchored and remembered that they had left their picnic hamper on the shore. The priest stepped out of the stern of the boat, and walking trustfully on the water, brought it back aboard. The minister then remembered the bag containing the cheese had been left behind so, equally believing in Christ's miracle, boldly stepped over the gunwhale and walked confidently over the gentle wavelets and rescued it; but most important of all, the whisky was still resting behind a stone. Not to be outdone, the corpulent Dean, jealous for the reputation of his Church, stepped cautiously out of the bow of the boat – and immediately sank to the bottom, followed by great bubbles of air, (smelling strongly of rich port) bursting on the surface of the loch.

"Perhaps we should have told him about the stepping stones," said the Priest, kindly.

"Ay, perhaps we should," said the minister, sadly shaking his head,

"Puir wee man."

So they both stepped overboard and brought back the crate of the "water of life" to console themselves.

A Highland lament, played on the pipes, up a lovely glen, is one of the most haunting and saddest sounds ever heard on earth. "To lament" is an interesting word, isn't it? Does it just mean to express infinitely mournful feelings about loss, or is there also a hint of the need to almost indulge in the sadness, to prolong it, to .express it, to work through the loss, instead of avoiding it, savouring the beauty of the departed? Is the word akin to "cathartic", the purifying of the emotions? It has been said of the Gaelic races that "their wars are merry and their songs are sad."

I remember the dominating figure of George MacLeod telling the guests about the background of this song, as we assembled in the refectory of Iona Abbey. He talked of Columba's men of the sixth century, as if he had been one of them; he spoke of their toiling steadily to the rhythm of their long oars as they rowed the wild seas of the Western Isles to tell of the victory of Christ over the powers of evil.

I bind this faith to me for ever,
By pow'r of faith, Christ's incarnation,
His baptism in the Jordan river,
His death on cross for my salvation;
His bursting from the spiced tomb,
His riding up the heavenly way,
His coming at the day of doom,
I bind until myself today
    From the hymn Come, ye faithful:
Ere he raised the lofty mountains,
Formed the sea or built the sky,
Love eternal, free and boundless
Moved the Lord of life to die,
Fore-ordained the Prince of princes
For the throne of Calvary.

At one of our parties in the garden, I included a couple who were going through a time of great sadness and worry. As they arrived, with many others, I greeted them warmly, but was not able to listen. As they were leaving I made sure that we had some time together; they brought me up to date with the difficulties, and then apologised about talking about such heavy things at a party.

"No, no," I said, "you've done right".

Before anybody had arrived I went through the list of guests invited, partly to remember their names, but mainly so that I could hold each one before God for a moment; and I asked Him to help me be especially sensitive to anybody who might be carrying some sort of a burden.

They were touched, the idea was new to them; but my wife Vici knew that this was natural for a priest.

This is the much loved prayer of St. Richard of Chichester. I would say it with all my heart to the great wooden cross on Good Friday:

Thanks be to thee, my Lord Jesus Christ,
for all the benefits thou has won for me,
all the pains and insults thou hast born for me.
Most merciful friend, redeemer and brother,
may I know thee more clearly,
love thee more dearly,
and follow thee more nearly,
day by day,

day by day.

This prayer was sung most beautifully in that wonderful, fresh, simple, personal Passion Play, Godspel.

• • •

Patience is a virtue
Find it if you can
Seldom in a woman,
Often in a man!

In the Western Isles the mountains are awe-inspiring, with the sea or the lochs winding among them. They can change from minute to minute; one moment the hills glow with the gentle or vivid purple of the heather, or blaze with the red gold of the dying sun. The next moment they become dark, under storm clouds and lashing rain. In the sea lochs the sea can be glassy calm, with the smallest and gentlest waves lapping the shore – a silence that can carry the lonely, haunting cry of a sea bird from a mile away. At other times great waves crack a hundred feet against the cliffs, hurling the spray high in the air; on these days you fear for the lives of anybody caught in those raging waters. The wind can then blow away the storm clouds in minutes, and as the sun begins to shine superb double rainbows appear over the sea and island.

Those are powerful descriptions of wild weather in the Islands in Robert Louis Stevenson's short story, "The Merry Men" – also in Peter May's detective novels set in the Outer Isles.

But not all is dramatic – there can be days on end of warm, breathless spiritless rain draining you of energy and bringing out the midges. No wonder that there are both high spirits and depression in the Highland and Island character.

Centuries ago, the men, women and children living in this magnificent, uplifting, dangerous landscape, grew their own way of being caught up in heaven. They lived by wresting forth oats from the thin soil, dependent on the health and the daily needs of their cattle. All too often the men fishing for food would be drowned in storms or ripping tides. In winter there would be weeks on end when the seas were too rough, the days too short for the men to brave the waves or the women to work in the little fields. The seed had been sown and now they just had to wait for spring. Spring comes later than in the South and after a longer, harsher winter, seems to bring a greater triumph of light over darkness, life over death.

They had to learn patience:

As it was,
As it is,
As it shall be
Evermore.
O Thou Trinity
Of grace!
With the ebb,

With the flow,
O Thou Trinity
Of grace!
With the ebb,
With the flow.

I am tired and I a stranger;
Lead thou me to the land of angels;
For me it is a time to go home,
To the Court of Christ, to the peace of heaven;
To the Court of Christ, to the peace of heaven.

These men and women were confident of the power of the Trinity to save them from the storms. Eternity was as real as the morning. The Saints were friends of Christ and friends of the people, Mary, Michael (Warrior Archangel), Bride (Bridget), Columba.

The prayers were born from hearth and home, from sea, from field, from loving, from birth, from death, from Eternity.

God bless Thyself my reaping,
Each ridge and plain and field,
Each ear a handful in the sheaf,
Each sickle curved, shaped, hard.
Each ear a handful in the sheaf.
Bless each maiden and youth,
Each woman and tender youngling,
Safeguard them beneath Thy shield of strength,
And guard them in the house of the saints;
Guard them in the house of the saints.
For the sake of Michael, head of hosts,

Of Mary fair skinned branch of grace,
Of Bride smooth-white of ringleted locks,
Of Columba of the graves and tombs,
Columba of the graves and tombs.

These prayers are sometimes known as Celtic spirituality; and it is no wonder that they have become so popular in recent years; there is more talk of the Resurrection than of the death of Christ; there is little doctrine, a wonderful blending of awe and easy friendship with the Almighty and, above all, no sense of ever-present heavy guilt. It is tragic that the ethos of the ancient Celtic Church was contaminated by the hierarchical legalism of the Roman Church and, centuries later, the heavy negative mood of Calvinism in Scotland.

It is interesting to notice the similarity between the Celtic Church and the Orthodox Churches of the East, with their sense of awe and undefined mystery.

• • •

I have a big stomach and narrow hips, so if I am not careful, my trousers are inclined to sag down to my knees. When visiting in my parish I would occasionally come out of the cottager of some attractive young wife and then be seen hitching up my trousers and re-buckling my belt. If somebody saw me, as they were passing by, I wondered what they might be thinking! Knowing my friends and parishioners, I could not assume that their thoughts would be innocent.

Two elderly Scots were playing golf – although it is misleading to use the word "playing" for a purposeful activity conducted in a grave and earnest manner worthy of the ancient competition.

At the ninth green, at the farthest end of the course, one of the stalwarts collapsed and died, his body lying between his opponent's ball and the hole. His lifelong friend took one look at him to confirm that he was dead, pulled him out of the way and finished his putt. He carried him to the Clubhouse and sadly shook his head; there was nobody to sign his card; sad, because he had scored his best round ever; he had put down his friend before taking each shot.

I was playing golf with a friend; I was just about to drive off when he suddenly said, in a broad accent, "Did I tell you that today my son is having an operation on his penis?" I was so startled that I topped the ball and it just rolled over the edge of the tee.

Last night I was trying to change the television channels; I pressed the buttons with the correct numbers, but nothing happened. I couldn't understand why until I saw that what I was holding in my hand was the telephone.

Last year Vici and I went on a cruise up the coast of Norway. It was late March, the snow lay thick upon the jagged mountains as we glided slowly by – the sun shone, the sky and sea were a vivid blue, making it one of the most strikingly beautiful sights which I have ever seen.

It was Holy Week, leading up to Easter. With the co-operation of the crew, I managed to hold three services in the bar, one on Palm Sunday, one on Good Friday and one on Easter Day. Growing numbers attended, ending up with over thirty. On the night before the first service I was sitting in the bar, chatting with an elderly couple. I told them of the service the following morning. The old lady's eyes filled with tears as she said,

"Like you, I didn't realise that it was Holy Week when I booked, and then I was really distressed when I found out. I brought my Prayer Book with me but it's not the same, reading the words on your own."

They were both deeply grateful. On Maundy Thursday, the previous year, she had been given the Maundy Money by the Queen, in recognition of her years of dedicated service for the Girl Guides and Children in Need. Good Friday happened to be also their Diamond Wedding Anniversary – 60 years. We blessed them and gave the collection to her two charities.

• • •

Sometimes I worry about the difficulties of encroaching old age, loss of balance, loss of breath, loss of memory – muddle – I had prepared Vici's cup of tea and the pot of food waste, - and then found myself walking up the garden to pour the tea into the compost bin.

In spite of my foreboding about the years ahead, I hope that I can accept the inevitable changes which will come. I think that acceptance is one of the qualities which the modern, secular world has lost. Because medical science is so amazing we are inclined to think that we are in control of our lives and our health; it is a form of human arrogance. In the great spiritual traditions of the world there is usually a true humility, however dubious the theology behind it, there is a simple acceptance of what is and what will be, whether the response of an Irish Catholic mother in old Ireland, on the loss of a child,

"Ah, well, it is the will of God,"

or the Muslim, "Imshalla.

I was strangely impressed to see on television hundreds of men in a mosque on one of the islands where thousands had perished in the tsunami – with one voice they were shouting "Allah Akbar", God is great. To our Western ears this is very strange, but it was humbling to see such defiance and confidence in the face of disaster.

This is the prayer which is said at meetings of Alcoholics Anonymous:

Lord,
Grant me the serenity to accept the things which I
    cannot change,

The courage to change the things which can be
    changed,
And the wisdom to know the difference.

It says it all, doesn't it?

At a wedding I often have intriguing
conversations with intelligent, questioning friends of
the bride and groom, while the champagne flows at
the reception. One agnostic son of a Vicar said,

"Why should I slavishly obey the voice of an
outside Being, instead of just following my own
conscience, and do what I believe right?"

"Perhaps, because your conscience may have
given up the unequal struggle?"

He grinned.

"Also, I believe that in obeying God you are not a
slave of a dictatorial, unpredictable tyrant, but that
you are 'obeying the needs and challenges of love',
God is love, and love is God, and God is in you, in
the people you are thinking about, and in everybody,
and everything, not only in this present moment, but
throughout all eternity. This may give a longer term,
more detached, more loving background to any of
your decisions?"

The young man looked thoughtful, but I don't
know whether he took in this massively different
understanding of God.

I was at a 60th birthday party in Milton Abbas. I
had enjoyed talking with the people I knew, and did

not have the energy to talk to strangers. I had collected my food and drink and looked for somewhere to sit and eat, but the only available chair was a deckchair – not easy to sit down in with a plate in one hand and a glass in the other! I handed the plate to somebody on my right and the glass to a man on my left, and sat down. Naturally, we started talking, and after a bit I said,

"Where are you from?"

"Australia".

"Ah …… which part?"

"Southern Australia".

"Yes, and which town?"

"Murray Bridge"

"I don't suppose, by any chance, you ever met my wife, Vici Martin, as she was then?"

He turned to his wife and said,

"Bev, this bloke is married to Vici!"

Not only were they friends of hers, but had been very good to her son David during his troubled times in his teens, and had attended his funeral after he had been tragically killed. They came and had lunch with us the next day. What are the chances of such a meeting? One in many millions? My grandmother would have said, "It was meant". It certainly was truly 'amazing' and 'wonderful', two words which are the meaning of the word, 'miracle'.

• • •

Tony Nott regularly takes me out sailing in his Shrimper. He has great affection for the red ensign which she wears on the stern. I respect its faded and tattered appearance, but disapprove of its size – it is far too small for such a noble little ship! Under pressure he has finally decided to buy a larger, more worthy ensign. We shall have a solemn laying up ceremony for the little rag, possibly with the help of a trumpet.

For some years, I have not dared to enjoy the wonderful experience of swimming from the boat; but this summer I was determined to go into the warm sea. I was just about to climb onto the ladder; Tony was releasing the life buoy and knocked the ensign into the sea. Knowing how important it was to him I shouted,

"I'll fetch it!" and lowered myself into the water and struck out for the wretched little thing as it drifted away.

"You're nearly there," said Tony untruthfully, "just a bit to the right".

I finally grabbed the thin flag pole and turned to hold it up for Tony to see .... the boat was already a hundred yards away, and getting further by the second

I had broken two of the cardinal rules which I had always emphasised to my guests on board:

Always swim towards the bow ....

Never swim after a light object being carried away by the tide.

I was only so stupid because I was grateful to Tony for taking me out so often ...... and, I suppose, because I wanted to show that I was still young and fit in spite of my many years!

I called out,

"You'll have to come and fetch me!"

I did not panic, because the sea was warm and I knew he would come. There would not be a headline in the local paper:

"77 year old Vicar swept out to sea, clutching something pink".

Tony started the engine, raised the anchor and circled round so I could grab the lifebuoy. All was well – until I reached the ladder on the boat, feeling fairly tired. The ladder sloped under the boat and I did not have the strength in my arms to haul myself up; Tony heaved until I stood precariously on the top step, but could not "get my leg over", and had to fall in.

Since then, the good man has adjusted the ladder; I had another wonderful warm swim and I walked up as if I were climbing the steps to a front door.

• • •

I often quote these words:

"It takes a brave man to believe, not that Jesus is like God, but that God is like Jesus; in other words, trust in God does not mean that an all-powerful Being will rescue you, but that life is about suffering, redeeming, vulnerable love."

Patriotism, love of your country, can turn into aggressive nationalism.

The spiritual path can turn into contempt and hatred of other faiths.

Fundamentalism, in any political party or religion, is one of the great dangers in the modern world if it is dogmatic, unquestioning, arrogant, in-human, both defensive and aggressive.

Whereas if I define a doctrine I make an enemy.

If I live a doctrine I make a friend.

• • •

I think this is enough of a rambling old man, so I will finish, before I find more and more, less and less interesting things to write ....so in the words of a blessing, I say, dear reader,

Go forth into the world in peace;
be of good courage;
hold fast that which is good;
render unto no man evil for evil;
strengthen the faint hearted,
support the weak,
help the afflicted,
honour all men;

love and serve the Lord,
rejoicing in the power of the Holy Spirit,
and the blessing of God Almighty,
Father, Son and the Holy Ghost
be with you, and all you love,
now and for evermore.
Amen